GW01606086

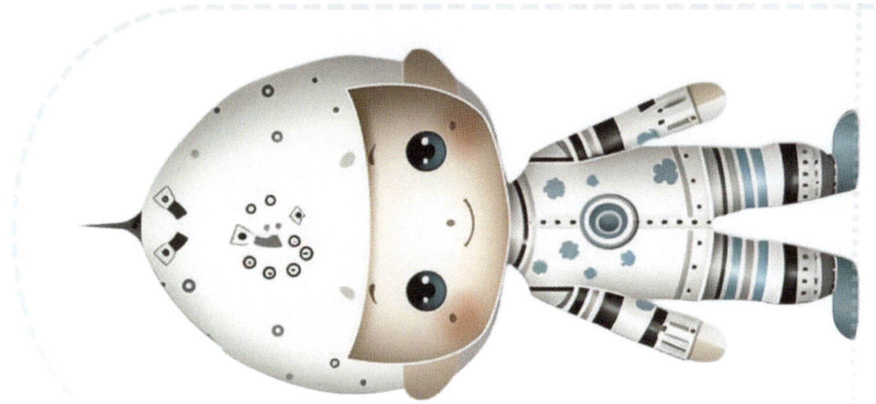

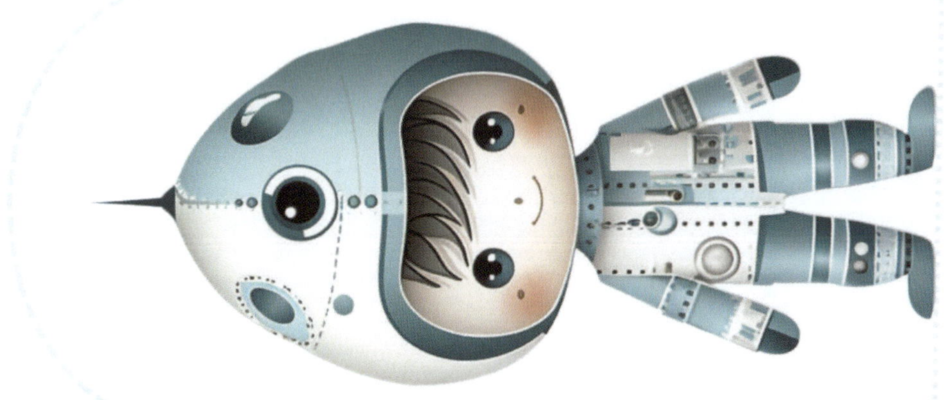

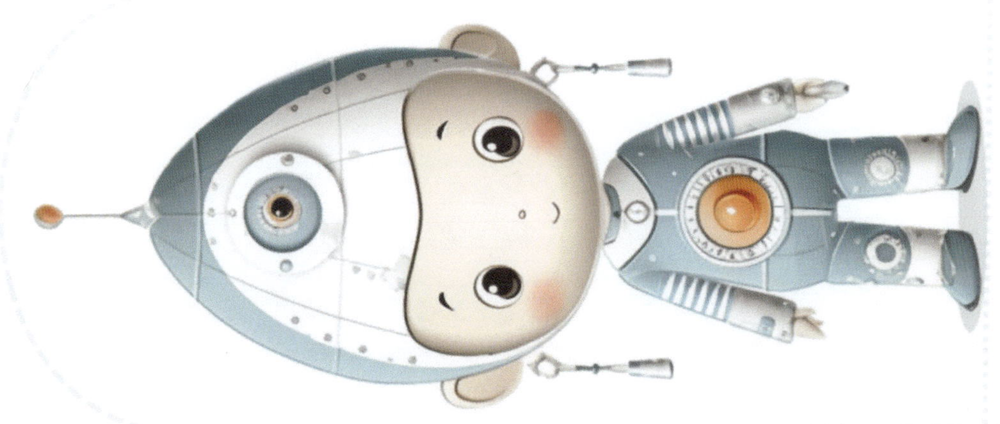

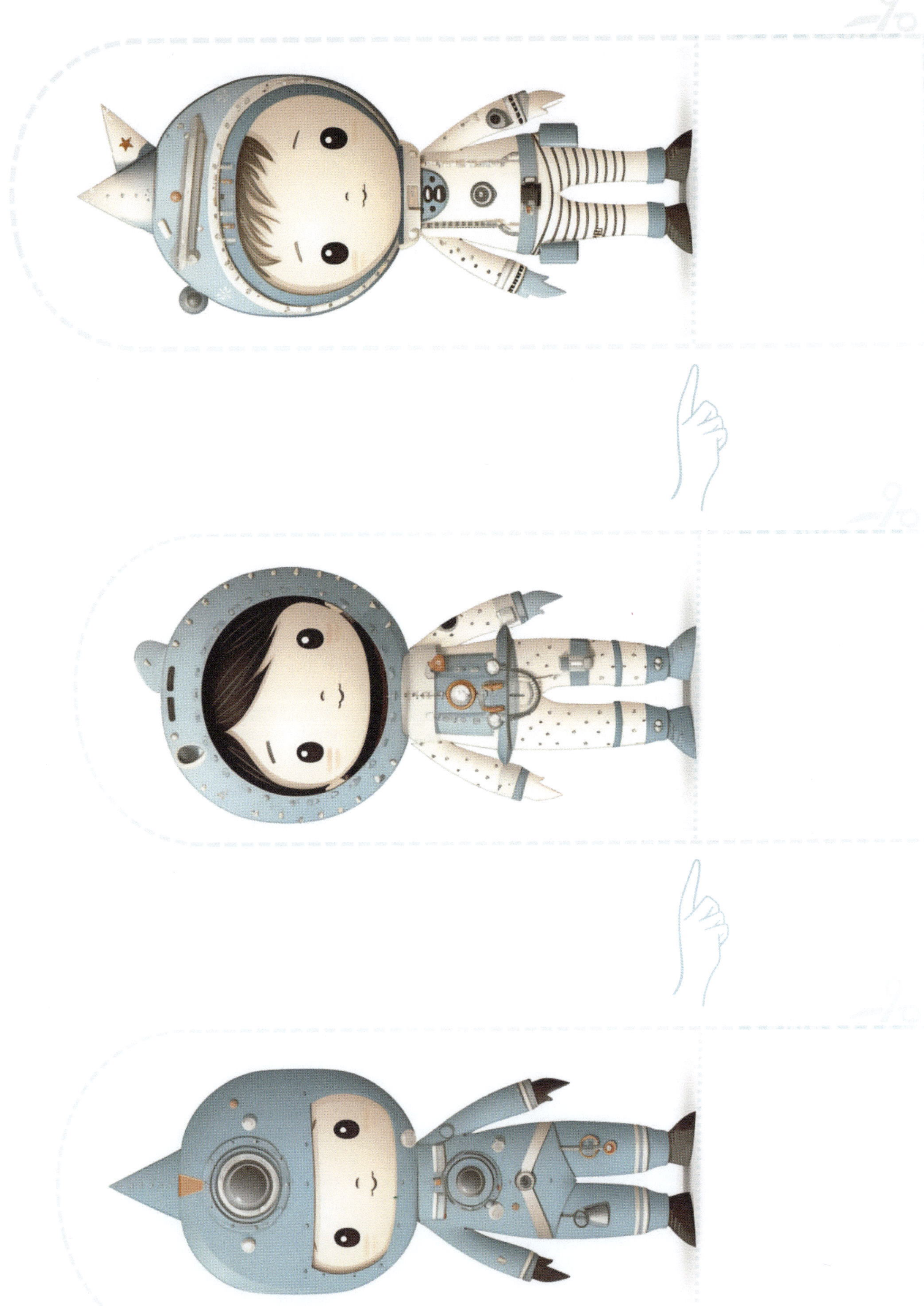

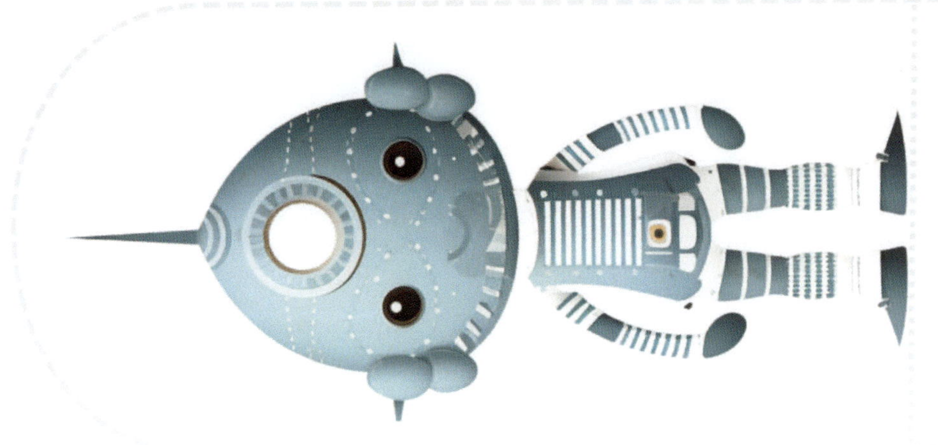

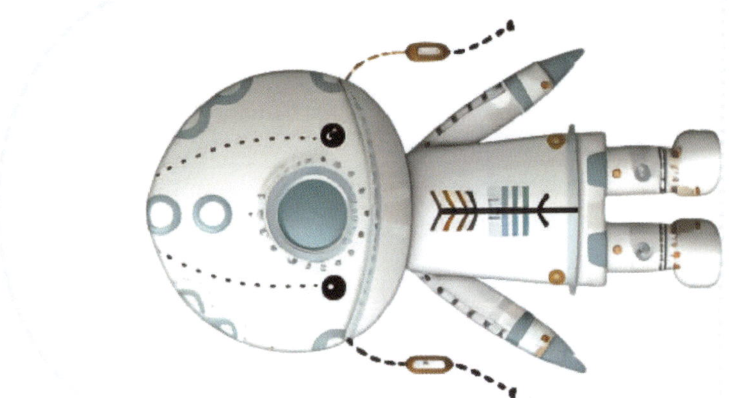

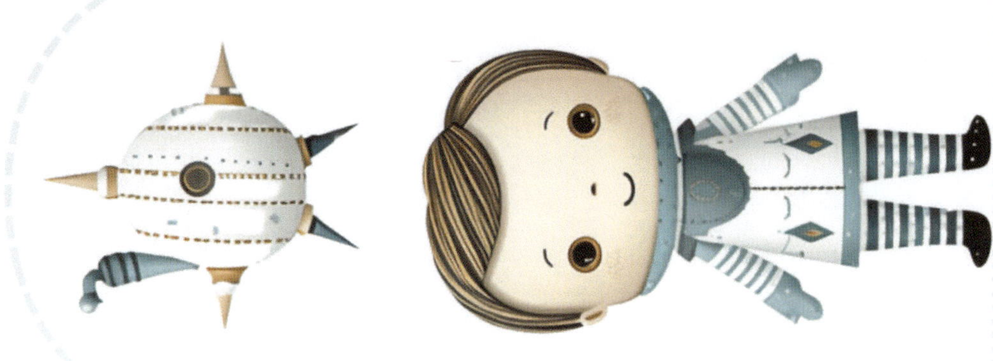

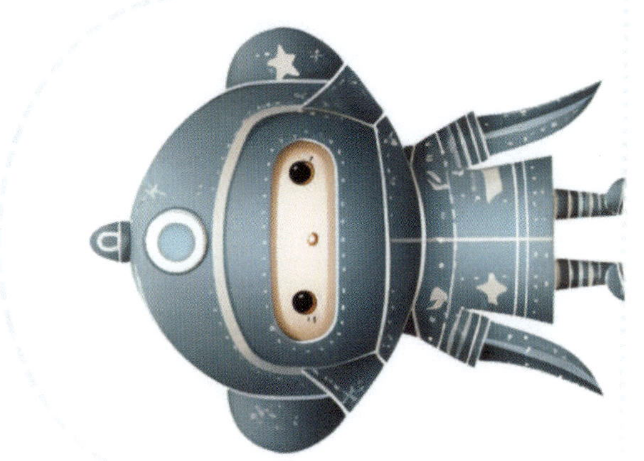

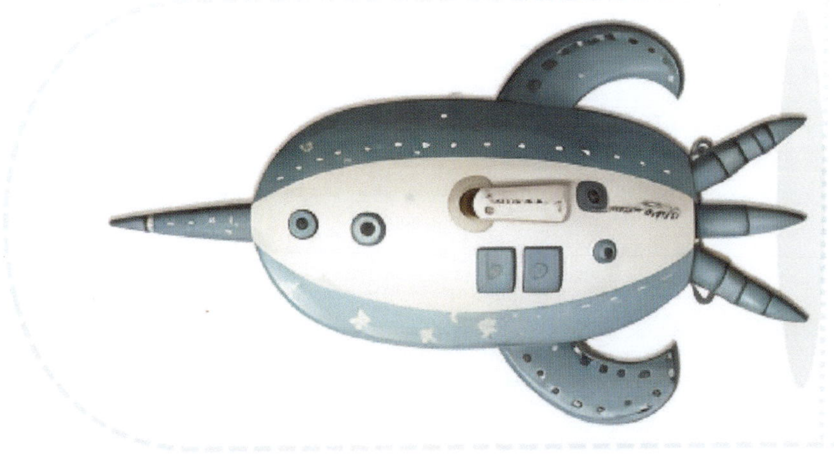

Step into the Enchanting Universe of

VINTAGE PAPER DOLLS

SERIES AVAILABLE NOW!

Easy Cut Out

PINK BLUSH VINTAGE PAPER DOLLS

WITH BACKDROP SETTINGS

9 UNIQUE DOLLS 7 BACKGROUNDS

Easy Cut Out

AZURE VINTAGE PAPER DOLLS

WITH BACKDROP SETTINGS

9 UNIQUE DOLLS 7 BACKGROUNDS

Easy Cut Out

FARMYARD FRIENDS PAPER DOLLS

WITH BACKDROP SETTINGS

9 UNIQUE DOLLS 7 BACKGROUNDS

Printed in Great Britain
by Amazon